Headline Series

No. 264   **FOREIGN POLICY ASSOCIATION** $3.00

HUMAN RIGHTS
and the
HELSINKI ACCORD
Focus on U.S. Policy
by William Korey

Introduction 5

1 From Yalta to Helsinki 8

2 The Meaning of Helsinki......................... 12

3 The Changing Posture
of the United States 24

4 Confrontation at Belgrade....................... 32

5 Madrid: Security vs. Human Rights........ 39

6 The Value of the Helsinki Process........... 51

Talking It Over..................................... 63
Annotated Reading List........................ 63

Cover design: Hersch Wartik

The Author

Dr. WILLIAM KOREY, director of international policy research of B'nai B'rith, recently studied the Helsinki process as guest scholar of the Woodrow Wilson International Center for Scholars in Washington, D.C. A graduate of the University of Chicago with an M.A. and Ph.D. from Columbia University, Dr. Korey taught history and international relations at CCNY, Brooklyn College and Columbia. He then shifted to the nongovernmental human rights field. A prolific writer, his major work is *The Soviet Cage: Anti-Semitism in Russia* (Viking). He also contributed to *Eleanor Roosevelt: Her Day* (New York Times/Quadrangle). Dr. Korey has been awarded fellowships by the Ford Foundation and the Carnegie Foundation.

The Foreign Policy Association

The Foreign Policy Association is a private, nonprofit, nonpartisan educational organization. Its purpose is to stimulate wider interest and more effective participation in, and greater understanding of, world affairs among American citizens. Among its activities is the continuous publication, dating from 1935, of the HEADLINE SERIES. The authors are responsible for factual accuracy and for the views expressed. FPA itself takes no position on issues of United States foreign policy.

HEADLINE SERIES (ISSN 0017-8780) is published five times a year, January, March, May, September and November by the Foreign Policy Association, Inc., 205 Lexington Ave., New York, N.Y. 10016. Chairman, Leonard H. Marks; Editor, Nancy L. Hoepli; Associate Editors, Ann R. Monjo and Mary E. Stavrou. Subscription rates, $12.00 for 5 issues; $20.00 for 10 issues; $28.00 for 15 issues. Single copy price $3.00. Discount 25% on 10 to 99 copies; 30% on 100 to 499; 35% on 500 to 999; 40% on 1,000 or more. Payment must accompany order for $6 or less. Second-class postage paid at New York, N.Y. POSTMASTER: Send address changes to HEADLINE SERIES, Foreign Policy Association, 205 Lexington Ave., New York, N.Y. 10016. Copyright 1983 by Foreign Policy Association, Inc. Composed and printed at Science Press, Ephrata, Pa.

Library of Congress Catalog No. 83-82291
ISBN 0-87124-082-3

Eleanor Roosevelt
(1884–1962)

This book is dedicated to Eleanor Roosevelt.

It marks the one-hundredth anniversary of her birth, a fact which seems a trick of time to those who remember her energy and presence in public affairs.

It marks the gratitude of the Foreign Policy Association to the young woman who, in 1928, was one of the incorporators of FPA.

Beyond the courteous ritual of a centennial dedication and the thoughtful gesture of a noted founder's memory, however, lies the deeper dedication.

It is the force of Eleanor Roosevelt's principles which continues to glow and illuminate our lives 21 years beyond her life. She had no vague hopes or naive wishes about humankind's necessities; she knew precisely what they were. Equality, liberty, social justice and democracy composed the cornerstones of her work. And she knew that their attainment could only come about if people were informed, organized and in operation.

Her constancy to these principles and the mechanisms they required were unflagging in her 50 years of public service. Her only nod to advancing age came in frequent rather shy references to donning a lace cap and sitting by the fire. They were uttered, one suspects, less out of anticipation of such an event than horror that mere age might take her out of the game while so much work remained.

It is particularly fitting that Dr. Korey's lucid explanation of the complexities of the Helsinki accord should be dedicated to Eleanor Roosevelt.

Although the accord came into being years after her death, its ongoing nature and substance embody the issues which energized her life.

She knew that war interrupted progress in human affairs and the accord's military sections aim to protect peace.

She knew that exchange of ideas, people, commerce across national boundaries promoted interdependence and reassurance of governments. A section of the accord speaks to those issues.

She knew that moving forward in human rights requires specificity, monitoring and accountability. The accord contains the framework to set those processes in motion.

And she knew that while it was difficult and tedious to incorporate political, diplomatic, economic and human affairs into one entity, it was essential to engage in the effort.

She knew, she acted, and she never gave up. It might have been enough to say simply:

To Eleanor Roosevelt

Patricia M. Derian,
President Jimmy Carter's
coordinator for human rights

Introduction

It was a decade ago, on July 3, 1973, that the structure which came to symbolize détente in Europe was created. Called the Conference on Security and Cooperation in Europe (CSCE), and comprising 33 countries of Europe as well as the United States and Canada, the new structure, it was hoped, would promote a greater sense of security by mitigating cold-war tensions and would eventually reduce—possibly remove—all barriers between the East and West.

What formally brought CSCE into existence was a resplendent and glittering meeting of 35 foreign ministers in the starkly beautiful Finlandia Hall of Helsinki. Not since the Congress of Vienna in 1815 which ended the Napoleonic epoch had so many foreign ministers gathered under one roof. For over four days the lofty and grand concert hall of the white granite building which seated the delegates and their aides echoed with speeches sounding the themes of détente. Not only were the North Atlantic Treaty Organization (NATO) and Warsaw Pact powers represented; every neutral and nonaligned country in Europe, however small, sent official delegates. Even tiny San Marino and Liechtenstein were present. Only Albania refused to participate.

Occupying center stage in the stellar gathering was Soviet Foreign Minister Andrei A. Gromyko. It was his speech that opened the session, and he had no hesitancy about speaking 50 minutes, twice as long as the agreed-upon time limit. Nor was it surprising that he assumed the leading role, for the conference was a Soviet idea whose time had come. At the core of the idea was the legitimization of Soviet domination of Eastern Europe through Western acceptance of post-World War II borders in that area. Gromyko at Helsinki hammered home the thesis of a code of conduct that would guarantee respect for "the territorial integrity of all European states *in their present frontiers*" (emphasis added). He also spoke at some length about the need for increased economic cooperation between Communist and capitalist countries.

Significantly, however, Gromyko said nothing about liberalizing daily contacts between the people of Eastern and Western Europe. This had been a NATO aim ever since 1966 when the West first began responding positively to Soviet soundings for a conference. In subsequent years, the West made Soviet acceptance of human rights and fundamental freedoms a condition for its acceptance of the postwar borders in Eastern Europe. At the preparatory discussions on a European security conference, the U.S.S.R. clearly signaled a willingness to accept the Western view and, specifically, to approve a greater degree of human contacts. Had the Kremlin retreated from its initial acquiescence by the time Gromyko addressed the Helsinki meeting?

It was British Foreign Secretary Sir Alec Douglas-Home who raised the issue in the sharpest form. "If we do not improve the life of ordinary people at the conference," he observed, "we shall be asked—and with justice—what all our fine words and diplomatic phrases have achieved." Sir Alec recalled the great hope of one of his predecessors, Ernest Bevin: "To be able to go down to Victoria Station in London, buy a ticket and go wherever I like without anybody demanding to see my passport."

The candor of the British carried the day as it swept like a fresh breeze across the marble corridors of Finlandia Hall. It was agreed to have three commissions covering, respectively, security, economic cooperation, and "humanitarian contacts," draw up recommendations for an agenda which would be discussed by the 35-member conference in Geneva, Switzerland, beginning in September.

In contrast to the toughness of the West Europeans, and especially the British, the U.S. presentation made by Secretary of State William P. Rogers was mild. While he supported the West Europeans and emphasized that human rights and freedoms were "a fundamental aspect" of the conference, he avoided challenging the U.S.S.R. or warning of negative repercussions should progress not be made on these matters. The White House, guided by national security adviser Henry A. Kissinger, looked upon the CSCE with considerable skepticism and perceived the human rights issue as unwarrantedly threatening to the Soviet Union at a time when Washington was pursuing its own bilateral détente with Moscow.

Today, a decade later, the United States is no longer a passive bystander. In fact it plays a central role in the CSCE and is its vigorous champion, especially in regard to human rights objectives.

The Soviet Union, on the other hand, is increasingly wary of the institution which, ironically, it helped bring into existence. Once enthusiastic about its creation, the Kremlin is striving desperately to reduce its human rights impact. Nonetheless, the institution remains, and its potential usefulness for Kremlin purposes has not altogether disappeared.

1

From Yalta to Helsinki

The road to Helsinki began at Yalta. As World War II approached its end in early 1945, the victorious allied wartime leaders, President Franklin D. Roosevelt, Britain's Prime Minister Winston Churchill and the Soviet Union's Premier Joseph Stalin, met in Yalta, a Crimean resort city. Their agenda called for resolving burning problems of territory and influence, as well as planning for the immediate future. The Red Army exercised decisive power throughout Eastern Europe and had begun installing Communist regimes in Bulgaria and Rumania. It did so despite prior agreements that provided for the establishment of allied control commissions to administer these countries. American and British commission members bitterly complained that they had been ignored by their Soviet counterparts. The question of Poland was even more pressing since the West had accorded support to the Polish exile government in London. Most critical was the future of Germany, as the allies made final military plans for the destruction of Nazi rule.

In January 1945, President Roosevelt privately told key U.S. senators that "the Russians had the power in Eastern Europe" and the "only practicable course was to use what influence we had to ameliorate that situation." If Soviet political and military preeminence in the region was to be recognized, Soviet adherence to certain basic standards of freedom and human rights would nonetheless be demanded. At Yalta, Roosevelt succeeded in winning approval for a "Declaration on Liberated Europe" which affirmed "the right of all people to choose the form of government under which they will live." The declaration also called for the creation of "interim governmental authorities broadly representative of all democratic elements in the population and . . . the earliest possible establishment through free elections of governments responsive to the will of the people."

Poland, too, was subjected to a compromise. It was agreed that the exile government in London would confer with a Red Army-sponsored regime in Lublin, Poland, in order to create a provisional administration. However, as Stalin later emphasized, the U.S.S.R. would consider its puppet regime in Lublin "the nucleus—that is to say, the principal part—of a new reorganized government of national unity." Still he pledged "free and unfettered elections as soon as possible on the basis of universal suffrage and secret ballots."

The future Polish borders were also discussed, with Stalin emphasizing that Soviet "security" was at stake "not only because we are on Poland's frontier but also because throughout history Poland has always been a corridor for attack on Russia." The allies agreed to move the Russian-Polish border a considerable distance westward, to the Curzon Line (the proposed armistice line between Poland and Russia that had been rejected after the Russo-Polish War of 1920), and to compensate Poland with undefined German territory. Later the Soviet regime absorbed the predominantly Ukrainian and Belorussian areas of eastern Poland and provided the latter with German regions up to the line formed by the Oder and Neisse rivers.

Two Germanys

The Yalta decision on Germany was dismemberment, with the creation of zones that largely reflected the prevailing respective military authority of Soviet, American and British occupation

armies. It was the Soviet Union that pushed especially hard for the division of Germany, although it was originally suggested by Roosevelt at the Teheran Conference of the allies in Iran in late 1943. Out of dismemberment eventually came a Western-oriented Federal Republic of Germany (or West Germany) and a Soviet satellite, the German Democratic Republic (or East Germany). Soviet military power later dictated the incorporation of some formerly German territory in East Prussia into the

U.S.S.R., just as it required that other areas up to the Oder-Neisse line be turned over to Poland and that Czechoslovakia again acquire the former Sudetenland.

Fear that the new territorial arrangement in Eastern and Central Europe might breed irredentism (a desire for reunification with others of the same ethnic or historic group)—especially among Germans—would haunt the Kremlin throughout the subsequent decades. For that reason it desperately sought formal Western approval of the frontiers. At the same time, security concerns together with Communist ideological demands led the Soviet Union to violate the various commitments it made at Yalta regarding free elections and fundamental freedoms throughout Eastern Europe. Each Communist regime under Soviet military domination (thus excluding Yugoslavia and later Albania) stamped out all freedoms and transformed itself into a totalitarian structure. When popular or even reform-minded governmental strivings for independence or freedom or human rights were expressed in Eastern Europe, the Kremlin simply crushed them by the use of overwhelming military force, as in Hungary in 1956 and Czechoslovakia in 1968.

Human Rights and Fundamental Freedoms

Human rights were seen by the Kremlin on an ideological level as something granted by the state when it chose to do so. The Soviet Union and its minions rejected the notion that human rights are inherent in the individual and that they are anterior to and superior to the state. Soviet Deputy Foreign Minister Andrei Y. Vishinsky underscored that view in his classic and historic confrontation with Eleanor Roosevelt on the eve of the vote on the Universal Declaration of Human Rights at the United Nations General Assembly in Paris on December 10, 1948. In her statement, Mrs. Roosevelt expressed the hope that the declaration of basic principles might well become the Magna Carta for all humanity.

It remained a Western hope to moderate the rigid totalitarian repressiveness through a more extensive degree of human contacts between East and West—a hope that found its expression in the Helsinki process.

11

2

The Meaning of Helsinki

As early as 1954 Soviet Foreign Minister V. M. Molotov had proposed an all-European treaty of collective security to assure the status quo in Eastern Europe. With the emergence a decade later of Soviet President Leonid I. Brezhnev as general secretary of the Communist party, the concept of a conference on security and cooperation in Europe began to take on its present form. In 1966, Brezhnev (along with Premier Alexei N. Kosygin) outlined specific proposals for the conference. The purposes were delineated as settling the German question, recognizing the postwar borders in Europe, developing cooperation, achieving arms reduction, and removing the presence of foreign (that is, U.S.) troops. The proposals were endorsed later that year by the Warsaw Pact.

The East's call for a dialogue did not fall upon deaf ears in the West. The fear of nuclear war, the growing trade relations between East and West, and a certain easing of tensions during the mid-'60s prompted a positive reaction. One critical stipulation, however, was made by NATO: the United States and Canada must be part of the conference. Even the Soviet invasion of Czechoslovakia in 1968 did not dampen Western enthusiasm.

While the United States remained skeptical, West European

interest intensified. West German Chancellor Willy Brandt's *Ostpolitik* (détente with the East) gave the interest a solid national basis. The formal NATO response, in 1969, to the Warsaw Pact's proposal mentioned for the first time that a European conference should deal with the subject of freer movement of peoples, information and ideas. The dialogue continued in 1970 through exchanges of communiqués between the Warsaw Pact and NATO, but there remained one major obstacle to the convening of a conference: the German question. Until that was settled, the allies would not agree to meet.

The signature of the Quadripartite Agreement on Berlin on September 3, 1971, was a crucial first step. It assured the Western presence in Berlin, the critical flashpoint of potential tension in Central Europe. It was followed the next year by "renunciation of force agreements" which West Germany reached with Poland and the U.S.S.R. A culminating treaty between West Germany and East Germany came at the end of the year. By then an accord between NATO (minus France) and the Warsaw Pact was completed for "mutual and balanced force reductions" (MBFR) talks covering Central Europe, to begin in 1973.

Soviet Retreat

With the German border issues for the time being resolved, the dialogue between East and West could move to a new level. Although the Soviet Union achieved its objective of assuring the borders of Eastern Europe, there still remained the task of obtaining NATO's sanction and legitimization of these arrangements, and Moscow pressed for an early establishment of the conference on security and cooperation in Europe. The Soviets' sense of urgency deepened as a Chinese-Soviet border conflict erupted in 1969. Under the circumstances, it was scarcely surprising that the U.S.S.R. would consent to NATO demands that the United States and Canada be included in the conference. The assent marked a sharp departure for Moscow, as one of its initial purposes in projecting a European security conference was to remove the American presence from Europe.

The principal recommendation to come out of the preparatory

CSCE CHRONOLOGY

Preparatory talks, Helsinki	November 1972–June 1973
Stage 1 Formal talks, foreign ministerial level: CSCE established	July 3–7, 1973
Stage 2 Working sessions, Geneva	September 1973–July 1975
Stage 3 Final Act signed, Helsinki	August 1, 1975
CSCE review meeting, Belgrade Preparatory meetings	June 15–August 5, 1977
Formal sessions	October 4, 1977–March 9, 1978
CSCE review meeting, Madrid Preparatory meetings	September 9–November 11, 1980
Formal sessions	November 11, 1980– September 1983

meetings was the establishment of the conference forum. Three stages were envisaged. The foreign ministers of the 33 countries of Europe plus the United States and Canada would meet briefly in Helsinki in July 1973 to constitute themselves as the Conference on Security and Cooperation in Europe. Stage 2 was to embrace a much longer period, as a detailed accord reflecting détente was worked out. The discussions would culminate in Stage 3 with a Final Act signed in solemn ceremony in Helsinki on August 1, 1975.

The Stage 2 deliberations continued for almost two years. As decisions could only be reached by consensus in closed discussions, the debates were heated and interminable and deadlocks not infrequent. Compromise was essential and the role of the neutral and nonaligned, especially Austria, Switzerland, Sweden, Finland and Yugoslavia, crucial. As they were not bound by the respective bloc security concerns, nor by the tendency of the blocs to reach a common position beforehand, they could approach questions in a more flexible and pragmatic manner.

The primary concern was the preparation of 10 fundamental principles that would guide interstate relationships (see page 16). For the Soviet Union and the other Warsaw Pact powers, the key draft principle was the "inviolability of frontiers" (Principle III), which was perceived as freezing the postwar status quo.

In two respects, however, the Soviets did not totally achieve their purpose. The Federal Republic of Germany, supported by the West, was insistent that "inviolability of frontiers" could not and must not preclude the reunification of the two Germanys by peaceful means. The U.S.S.R. refused to have any modification introduced into the principle itself but did agree to a "floating sentence" whereby "frontiers can be changed in accordance with international law by peaceful means and by agreement" between participating states. That idea was eventually incorporated into Principle I, dealing with sovereignty and equality of states. On the eve of the signing of the Helsinki Final Act, the West German foreign minister, Hans-Dietrich Genscher, announced that "the conference has not finalized the status quo in Europe. And what the conference did not do by texts we should not do by words."

Second, the "self-determination of peoples," which allows "all peoples . . . to determine, when and as they wish, their internal and external political status without external interference. . ." was enshrined in Principle VIII. This principle was vigorously opposed by the U.S.S.R. In its view, this right should be associated with the aspirations of colonial peoples, not the peoples of Europe. The West insisted upon keeping the principle not only to permit the possible reunification of the Germanys but to preclude the reapplication of the Brezhnev Doctrine. That doctrine sanctioned Soviet military intervention that eliminated Czech party leader Alexander Dubcek's striving for self-determination, for "communism with a human face," in 1968.

The West's basic striving was summed up in Principle VII: "Respect for human rights and fundamental freedoms, including the freedom of thought, conscience, religion or belief." For the

FINAL ACT
(also known as the Helsinki agreement or accord)
of the
Conference on Security and Cooperation in Europe (CSCE)
signed August 1, 1975

Basket One:
- Declaration of Principles
  - I Sovereign equality, respect for the rights inherent in sovereignty
  - II Refraining from the threat or use of force
  - III Inviolability of frontiers
  - IV Territorial integrity of states
  - V Peaceful settlement of disputes
  - VI Nonintervention in internal affairs
  - VII *Respect for human rights and fundamental freedoms, including the freedom of thought, conscience, religion or belief* (emphasis added)
  - VIII Equal rights and self-determination of peoples
  - IX Cooperation among states
  - X Fulfillment in good faith of obligations under international law
- Deals with confidence-building measures relating to European military security

Basket Two
- Deals with economic, scientific, technical and environmental cooperation, emphasizing the development of East-West trade, the planning of joint research projects, and increased tourism

Basket Three
- Deals with cooperation in humanitarian and other fields, specifically advocating the freer movement of ideas, information, and people through family reunification, increased access to broadcast and printed information, and increased educational and cultural exchanges

first time in history, human rights were formally recognized in an international agreement as a fundamental principle regulating relations between states.

The principle incorporated three concepts alien to Soviet tradition and practice and, therefore, set a major standard toward which the populace in Eastern Europe might aspire. One was "the inherent dignity of the human person. . . ." It was introduced by Switzerland to express the Western concept that human rights are inherent in the human condition and not simply a privilege extended by the state.

The second concept established, if somewhat indirectly, the link between détente and human rights. The text described human rights as "an essential factor for the peace, justice and well-being necessary to ensure the development of friendly relations and cooperation. . . ." The formulation reversed the hierarchical priorities of the Communist world which made all progress and relationships dependent upon détente.

Thirdly, the principle offered the people of totalitarian and authoritarian regimes, in which the state commands the media and determines what information is appropriate, the revolutionary notion that an individual has a right "to know and act upon his rights. . . ." Once grasped in Eastern Europe, the idea could constitute a potentially explosive challenge to the authorities.

Basket Three

Equally important, in terms of human rights, was Basket Three of the Final Act. (The act has three parts, known as baskets, a term coined by the Netherlands.) Basket One contained the 10 principles and also dealt with confidence-building measures to promote security. Basket Two was concerned with the advancement of trade. Basket Three, in contrast to the other two, was exclusively a Western proposal aimed at fulfilling the aspiration of "freer movement of peoples and ideas."

The centerpiece of Basket Three was the human contacts section in which the key phrase was "reunification of families," a euphemism for emigration—at least with respect to family and kin. Final Act signatories pledged themselves to "deal in a positive and humanitarian spirit with persons who wish to be reunited with members of their family." Signatories were further obliged to "facilitate" and "expedite" the granting of visas, to charge only moderate sums for visas, and to refrain from reducing or removing the rights of those seeking to emigrate. The significant implications of this language for East European governments are self-evident.

Linkage: Human Rights and Security

As important as the incorporation of human rights obligations in the Final Act was the linkage of such obligations to other aspects of the accord. The act stipulated that all of its 10 principles are of "primary significance and, accordingly, they will be equally and unreservedly applied, each of them being interpreted taking into account the others. . . ." None of the baskets, whether security, trade or human rights, is to be considered as more important than the other two.

Linkage was perceived as being at the very heart of détente. This is reflected in the history of the Final Act. The decision to create a CSCE was a trade-off between security and human rights. And the discussions of 1972–75 were an endless series of bargaining sessions revolving around these considerations. Clearly, human rights were accepted as a vital part of the international agenda. However, Soviet acceptance did not come easily or quickly.

The first major threat to the human rights clauses was a Soviet attempt to use the language of Principle I, covering sovereignty and rights inherent in sovereignty which enable a state to determine its own "laws," "regulations" and "cultural systems," in the preamble to Basket Three. The aim was patently self-evident: to the extent that Soviet laws, regulations and customs were not in consonance with Basket Three provisions, the latter were nullified.

The West, with U.S. encouragement, resisted. The delegation from Finland worked out a key compromise which provided for a preambular insert that made specific reference to Principle I on sovereignty. Since the West, and especially the neutrals, were concerned about the possible misuse of the Finnish compromise by Moscow, they pressed successfully for new language, sponsored by Sweden, in Principle X. While the signatories are granted the right to determine their own laws, they are nonetheless obligated to "pay due regard to and implement the provisions of the Final Act of CSCE. . . ."

The second Kremlin attempt at circumscribing the human rights provisions was made in connection with Principle VI on nonintervention in internal affairs. Western negotiators had tried to shape the principle so that it would be limited to intervention by some form of coercion. (In this connection, it should be emphasized that the West was intent upon having the Final Act carry a strong statement on nonintervention if only to nullify, from an international law standpoint, the Brezhnev Doctrine.) A delicate balance in the wording was essential to serve different purposes.

The text of the Final Act's Principle VI ended up by carrying the term "coercion," which was perceived as clarifying what was meant by "intervention." Thus diplomatic representations or other forms of government complaints about violations of Basket Three provisions could be legitimized on grounds that these could hardly be described as "coercion." But even with this insertion, the Soviets were not prevented later from attempting to use the principle of nonintervention to neutralize the human rights provisions.

The third Soviet effort focused upon the lengthy title of Principle VII, "Respect for human rights. . . ," etc. The U.S.S.R. deliberately supported the language of the title because it would parallel the language of Article 18 of the International Covenant on Civil and Political Rights, adopted by the United Nations General Assembly in 1966. That particular article established sharp limitations on the exercise of freedom on grounds of protecting "public safety, order, health, or morals or the fundamental rights and freedom of others." Moscow tried—but failed—to use the escape clauses of the covenant to weaken the human rights provisions. Nonetheless, later on, the Kremlin would cite the covenant's escape clauses to justify abridgment of

freedom—even though these clauses are themselves under severe legal limitations and are not intended to restrict the purpose of the covenant.

A Legally Binding Document?

The U.S.S.R., even if defeated on human rights issues, clearly did not view the adopted clauses as a threat for the foreseeable future and felt that the Final Act, as a whole, was a major historic contribution to its strategic objectives. This is evidenced by the intriguing position it took on the status of the Helsinki accord under international law. A key and burning question at the CSCE meetings was whether the Helsinki Final Act was to be a legally binding document. While almost all delegations thought that the Final Act clauses should be considered *morally* compelling, they did not initially see them as *legally* binding. As the negotiations proceeded, more and more enthusiasm was registered by the delegates for an emphasis upon language that at least implied, if it did not specify, a legally binding instrument. The trend was a cause of concern to the U.S. delegation, which was keenly aware of the predisposition of Congress to question the right of the President to conclude important international agreements without congressional consent. Moreover, and far more significantly, the White House was, at most, quite indifferent to the Final Act. A legally binding treaty was the last thing desired.

It was the British who used the phrase Final Act (later taken up by the Netherlands)—instead of covenant or treaty—in order to create the presumption that the document was intended to be a legally nonbinding instrument.[1] Nonetheless—and strikingly—the U.S.S.R. chose to regard it as virtually having a juridically

Michael Witte, *Time,* 1977

binding character. At Helsinki, Brezhnev declared his assumption that all the countries "will implement the undertakings reached" and, as for the U.S.S.R., "it will act precisely in this manner." The statement was repeated almost verbatim in a government announcement issued on August 6. Two days later, *Izvestiya* (the Soviet daily) declared that the Helsinki principles should be "made a law of international life" which is not to be breached by anyone.[2]

Did the Soviet emphasis on the binding character of the Final Act apply to the human rights clauses? Brezhnev himself appeared to have second thoughts about the question when he met, two weeks after Helsinki, with 18 American congressmen in Yalta. He was quoted as distinguishing between some provisions of Helsinki which have "a binding nature" and others which will be "fulfilled according to agreements reached on the part of the [participating] states." Only "as time goes on," he observed, would the fulfillment be realized "according to agreements."

The Brezhnev distinction was raised two days later by a U.S. presidential aspirant, Terry Sanford, at the time visiting Premier Kosygin in the Kremlin. Sanford reported that Kosygin rejected any distinction, and he "went to some length to stress that they intended to be bound by the total agreement." The distinction appeared to be dropped by Brezhnev himself at a Congress of the Polish Communist party in December 1975. He told his audience that "we stand for putting into practice the concrete points of the Final Act."

The Kremlin not only pressed for a legally binding interpretation of the Final Act; it sought to give the CSCE a permanent institutional form. It had in mind some kind of European security council which would be serviced by a permanent secretariat operating from a permanent headquarters. The secretariat, presumably, would have numerous functions, including the issuance of regular reports on implementation.

Even as the West, and especially the United States, was reluctant to accept the Final Act as a binding agreement, so was it suspicious about any institutionalization of CSCE. From its perspective, the creation of permanent central organs, including those dealing with security, would have given Moscow a toehold in Western defense matters. Moreover, the institutionalization was seen as a possible Soviet device to eventually exclude the United States from Europe, or reduce its impact.

Review-Meeting Compromise

Denmark proposed a compromise in the form of "review meetings" which would "continue the multilateral process" through a "thorough exchange of views" on the "implementation of the provisions of the Final Act" and on programs for "deepening" mutual relations, "improvement" of security, and "development" of both cooperation and "the process of détente in the future." Only one review meeting was specified—that in Belgrade, Yugoslavia—but this one would "define the appropriate modalities for the holding of other meetings." What was seen as a modest device for blunting Soviet insistence upon institutionalization ultimately became a procedure which the West would use effectively and about which the U.S.S.R. has become increasingly wary and even hostile.

At the time, according to a State Department official who had been in charge of CSCE matters, "we didn't know what we were doing." No one, he recalls, understood clearly what the words of the Danish proposal meant. Especially unclear was the term "review."

The Soviet attempt to institutionalize the Helsinki agreement was part of a broader Kremlin objective to make the idea and practice of détente irreversible. This was resisted by the West, which was determined to describe détente as a preliminary step in a *process* of improving relations between groups of states and peoples. The delegations from Britain, Italy and the Netherlands were in the forefront of this aim, and they ultimately prevailed. The text of the key preamble of Basket One reads: "*Convinced* of the need to exert efforts to make détente both a continuing and an increasingly viable and comprehensive process, universal in scope, and that the implementation of the results of the CSCE will be a major contribution to this process. . . ."

The language gave the Helsinki Final Act a dynamic quality which could be reinforced and given expression by the follow-up review meetings. Such dynamism could and would have enormous ramifications. History offers instances of international agreements producing consequences totally unanticipated and reversing the role of the major parties to the agreement. The Helsinki accord would constitute an archetype.

---

[1]Determined to make patently clear the nonbinding character of the Final Act, the U.S. delegation as well as the British supported a West German clause stipulating that the instrument is not a treaty susceptible to registration under Article 102 of the UN Charter.

The U.S.S.R., Switzerland and Rumania resisted the West German initiative as unnecessarily denigrating the results of the conference. These countries proposed that the language in the accord should define only what the Final Act was, not what it was not. A compromise proposal provided for a paragraph which "requested" Finland to transmit the Final Act to the UN secretary-general. The paragraph would add that the act "is not eligible for registration under Article 102 of the Charter of the UN. . . ."

[2]The most precise Soviet statement on the juridical character of Helsinki was made in the Soviet journal *New Times* (November 1975) by a well-known Soviet commentator, Valentin Yaroslavtsev. He said "the signatures affixed to the Final Act have also a legal significance—they made it a binding international document." The firmness of the Soviet legal commitment was given special emphasis in the closing communiqué of the meeting between French President Valéry Giscard d'Estaing and Brezhnev in Moscow in October 1975. They declared "their resolve to observe strictly and to implement in all fields" the principles of Helsinki. They also expressed their intention "to implement fully all the provisions of the Final Act," including those in the humanitarian fields.

3

The Changing Posture
of the United States

The United States assumed a publicly passive role in the early Helsinki talks. Kissinger, at the time national security adviser, saw America's role as one of slowing down the process and limiting the damage once the negotiations had begun. Although Kissinger viewed the discussions with great skepticism and favored avoiding the human rights issue, it would be an error to assume total American indifference, as has been suggested in various commentaries on the early history of the CSCE.

The deputy head of the U.S. delegation to the preliminary talks in Helsinki in 1972, George S. Vest played a very active, if behind-the-scenes, role. Indeed, the meetings of Western as well as neutral and nonaligned representatives in the Basket Three discussions actually took place in the Helsinki headquarters of the American delegation. The general policy directive which Vest was given by the State Department was to extend as much cooperation as possible on human rights to America's European friends.

As the CSCE meetings moved from the preparatory stages to formal conference deliberations in 1973–75, the United States continued the earlier pattern. According to a knowledgeable source who later served as head of the U.S. delegation, Ambassador Albert W. Sherer Jr., the Americans had "a small but active and influential delegation. . . . We were passive in the sense that we urged them [NATO] to take the lead in public discussion." He added that the U.S. delegation was "active behind the scenes, especially in our relations with Warsaw Pact delegations." Besides concentrating their attention on the East European delegates, the U.S. officials "were helpful across the board" with the neutral and nonaligned delegations.

U.S. delegation members, according to Sherer, were "given a free hand." He remembers that "very, very few instructions were ever sent by telegram or letter" from Washington. There was but one oral instruction which was general in nature: "You know what you are supposed to do, don't louse it up!"

With time Kissinger shed his more pronounced anxieties about the Helsinki process and even warmed to the subject. On several occasions when key human rights issues were stalemated, he played a positive role. In bilateral talks with Gromyko, Kissinger's intervention was helpful, and indeed, during the very last stages of the discussions, it was crucial.

Still, the United States scarcely exercised the leadership role which should have been warranted by its power, its importance in NATO, and its traditional commitment to human rights. Of the literally thousands of formal proposals advanced at the Helsinki-Geneva talks, only one or two were American in origin. According to Luigi Vittorio Ferraris in *Report on a Negotiation,* America's role was primarily one of "detachment."

At the handsomely mounted and large-scale summit ceremony on August 1, 1975, when the Final Act was signed, President Gerald R. Ford represented the United States. Kissinger had not been enthusiastic about the President's participating, and the State Department made a deliberate and determined effort to play down the Helsinki meeting among the media. The downgrading was, in part, a response to the prevailing unpopularity of the Helsinki agreement in both conservative and moderate circles. They saw the accord as a betrayal of the people of Eastern Europe, a perception that was vigorously and publicly pushed by

Soviet dissident author Alexander Solzhenitsyn, at that time already living in the West. Key newspapers and journals urged Ford not to attend. The White House mail ran 10–1 against his participation. Ronald Reagan strongly opposed his going as did Senator Henry M. Jackson (D-Wash.). Former Under Secretary of State George W. Ball summed up conventional wisdom by calling the Helsinki accord "a defeat for the West."

U.S. About-face

By the beginning of 1977, a radical transformation in the U.S. posture had taken place. From a largely passive, low-profile role, the United States moved to a very active, high-profile position, especially with respect to human rights. Four factors contributed to this extraordinary change: (1) intrinsic Helsinki Final Act features that gave the process high visibility; (2) the impact of the Helsinki accord upon the people of Eastern Europe; (3) the creation in the United States of a unique institution, the U.S. Commission on Security and Cooperation in Europe; and (4) the unprecedented human rights thrust of the new Carter Administration.

The implementation process provided for in the Final Act inevitably drew public attention to review meetings. This meant that the U.S. posture could no longer be shielded behind closed diplomatic discussions but rather was exposed to public view. Moreover, as the President's first report on the Helsinki accord indicated, the United States "believed it important for the President . . . to have a public forum for the proclamation of our values to all the peoples of Europe." International public forums are not easily dismissed.

Did the U.S.S.R. anticipate the consequences of public forums dealing with implementation? Evidently not. A State Department expert who had participated in the negotiations on Basket Three recalls that the Soviet delegates believed that fulfillment of the Helsinki human rights provisions would involve a long period—10 to 15 years. Indeed, several initial Soviet steps taken to meet the aims of the Final Act suggest that the Kremlin did not expect any threatening repercussions from the human rights provisions.

The publication of the full text of the Final Act in *Izvestiya* was to prove profoundly enlightening to the democratic dissidents and activists. Plans were advanced by the authorities to incorporate the 10 principles of the Helsinki accord, including the human rights principle, into the new Soviet constitution. Moreover, the U.S.S.R. adopted in 1976 a series of measures easing emigration procedures in keeping with Basket Three.

The consequent relaxation in emigration rules was to exert a significant impact upon several ethnic groups within the U.S.S.R. that had been and were continuing to seek reunion with their kin abroad—especially Jews, ethnic Germans and Armenians. During the next several years, the emigration rate of these groups rose markedly. The procedures, however, were not designed to apply to the Soviet population generally. The U.S.S.R. does not recognize the absolute right of emigration but rather restricts it largely to ethnic groups whose homeland is elsewhere. Armenians are treated as a special case. They have been allowed to reunite with kin in the United States. Jews or Germans who were allowed to emigrate, in contrast, were given visas specifically for Israel and the Federal Republic of Germany, respectively.

Helsinki Monitors

Especially noteworthy was the appearance, beginning in May 1976, of voluntary Helsinki Watch Committees, first in Moscow and then in Leningrad, Kiev, Vilnius, Tbilisi and Yerevan. These groups, guided by "the right of the individual to know and act upon his rights," as spelled out in Principle VII of the Final Act, proceeded to establish study methods for monitoring official compliance with the Final Act. The bold and unprecedented action could not but stir anxiety in the narrowly rigid Soviet security organs. Immediately after the Moscow group's first public announcement, in which it said it would report to the Helsinki accord signatories "direct violations" of the Final Act's human rights provisions, the group was declared to be "an illegal organization" engaged in "provocations." Yet it was not until March 1977, almost 10 months after the first Watch Committee was launched, that the regime moved to eliminate them. The delay testified to the fact that the Kremlin scarcely anticipated the potentiality of public action flowing from the Helsinki Final Act.

Similar monitoring groups began springing up elsewhere in Eastern Europe. In January 1977, 300 persons signed "Charter 77," a Czechoslovak human rights manifesto which spoke of the intent "to work individually and collectively for respect for human and civil rights in Czechoslovakia and the world" in accordance with "rights provided for . . . in the Final Act of the Helsinki conference. . . ." In Poland, a Committee on Workers' Self-Defense (KOR) was created, calling for the extension and protection of human rights in Poland. Ultimately, the great mass movement of Solidarity would emerge in Poland. One of the basic objectives upon which it insisted was government adherence to the Helsinki accord.

Clearly, the Helsinki accord had unexpectedly kindled new hopes and sparked human rights demands throughout Eastern Europe. Initially, because the Final Act seemed to sanction Soviet territorial and political aspirations in Eastern Europe, many in the Soviet dissident movement saw it as a betrayal of their interests. Andrei Sinyavsky recalls that he wept bitter tears when he read the text. The consequences in the real world, however, proved to be quite different. The Helsinki accord had become a powerful weapon to expose human rights abuses.

The dimensions of public monitoring activity prompted a strong negative response by the Soviet Union and its satellites in Eastern Europe, especially Czechoslovakia. The arrests of the head of the Moscow group, Yuri Orlov, and of one of its principal members, Anatoly Shcharansky, acquired particular notoriety. The suppression of Charter 77 in Czechoslovakia similarly evoked dismay.

The U.S. Helsinki Commission

Both the emergence of active democratic groups in Eastern Europe and their suppression had a powerful impact on U.S. public opinion. The former demonstrated the value and potential usefulness of the Helsinki Final Act. What would emerge from this keen awareness is an extraordinary and unprecedented public body comprising members from the legislative and executive branches—the U.S. Commission on Security and Cooperation in Europe. Its primary function was to monitor compliance with the provisions of the Helsinki accord dealing with human rights. The commission was a major driving force for changing the American posture to one of leadership.

Shortly after the Helsinki Final Act was signed, Congresswoman Millicent Fenwick and Senator Clifford P. Case, both Republicans from New Jersey, introduced legislation to create the unique instrumentality of the commission. Mrs. Fenwick considered that a purely legislative group, whether committee or subcommittee, would fail to reflect the character of the Final Act. The monitoring body, she believed, should include representatives of all government bodies responsible for implementing the accord—and thus representatives should come from the Departments of State, Defense and Commerce, along with members of Congress.

Hearings were held on the proposed legislation in 1975 and again in 1976 by a subcommittee of the House Foreign Affairs Committee. Vigorous support came from numerous nongovernmental organizations as well as from various members of Congress. The House endorsed the legislation on May 17 by a lopsided vote of 240–95. On May 21, the Senate acted favorably.

The legislation created a 15-member commission—12 from the Congress (6 from each chamber), the other 3 to be appointed by the executive branch. Although conceived as a joint legislative-executive group, the power clearly weighed on the legislative side. From Kissinger's perspective the legislation was anathema with respect to both the human rights thrust and legislative assertiveness in foreign affairs. Letters were sent from the White House and the State Department stating that the monitoring of the Helsinki accord was properly an executive-branch function.

President Ford signed the legislation on June 3, 1976, but, at the same time, noted that executive appointments to the commission would be confined to observer, not member, status. He indicated his concern about potential constitutional and policy problems raised by executive-branch participation. The Depart-

Congressman Dante B. Fascell (r.), chairman of the U.S. Helsinki commission, and Senator Claiborne Pell with Avital Shcharansky, wife of imprisoned Moscow Helsinki Watch monitor.

ment of Justice was reported to have found no constitutional problem, on the basis that the commission wielded no power. Its role was reserved for monitoring through studies, holding hearings and issuing reports. The newly appointed chairman of the commission, Congressman Dante B. Fascell (D-Fla.), stressed at the first formal meeting that he saw no constitutional problems resulting from the composition or tasks of the commission.

Press reaction to the commission's establishment in Western Europe was generally positive. Its study mission to 18 West European countries received a favorable assessment. The group reported that in Western Europe there was virtual unanimity with the view that the Helsinki accord had "already been more productive than Western signatories anticipated. . . ." Not surprisingly, the media in Eastern Europe reacted angrily, criticizing the notion that a congressional group would attempt to be the arbiter of who is, or is not, adhering to the provisions of the Helsinki accord. This was declared to be interference in the internal affairs of state.

Carter on Human Rights

With Carter as President, the commission came into its own. The relationship between the two became symbiotic, each reinforcing the other. One week after his election, Carter said that "consummation of the Helsinki agreement concerning human rights would be an ever-present consideration" in his foreign policy. Congressman Fascell would help drive home the theme of human rights. At a meeting of President-elect Carter with his foreign policy transition team, including various congressmen, at the Smithsonian Institution, Carter spoke about the need for a moral policy without referring to the words "human rights." Fascell spoke up: human rights must be a "major component" of American policy. He was vigorously supported by Senator Hubert H. Humphrey (D-Minn.). The intervention of the elder statesman was decisive.

Carter asked Fascell for "talking points" in the preparation of his inaugural address. Among them was human rights. It became the centerpiece of the address and of the new Administration. Just prior to the inauguration, in January 1977, the new Secretary of State Cyrus R. Vance met with Fascell to discuss the forthcoming review meeting of the Helsinki signatories. At this crucial meeting, Vance agreed that the review meeting focus on implementation. He also agreed to integrate the commission into the delegation which would go to Belgrade.

4

Confrontation
at Belgrade

The U.S. posture at the first review meeting in Belgrade was signaled by President Carter in his address to the NATO council in London in May 1977. He emphasized that the United States would insist upon "a careful review of progress by all countries in implementing all parts" of the Helsinki accord. To give expression to both the new leadership role of the United States and the focus upon human rights, the Carter Administration chose an outstanding public figure who had served as a prominent justice of the U.S. Supreme Court and later as the U.S. ambassador to the UN—Arthur J. Goldberg. Moreover, in the public arena, Goldberg had been a leading advocate of human rights. Virtually all the other chief delegates had come from their respective professional diplomatic corps, and none occupied particularly prominent positions.

Prior to Belgrade, the Kremlin began to make clear that it would not be the "whipping boy of Helsinki" on the human rights issue. Détente, the Soviets contended, would be undermined were Belgrade to become "the scene of a propagandist wrangle" or a "complaints court" or a "tribunal." The Soviets would strive, Moscow indicated, to have any review of the past rejected. If some kind of formal review was demanded by the Final Act, then, at best, the review should only take the form of each delegation accounting for its own country's "track record," with no discussion of implementation by another country. It was the future to which the Belgrade meeting should address itself. To one Western critic, the Soviet tactic was one of "escape forward" in order to avoid international scrutiny of compliance.

In view of the Soviet Union's adamant opposition to a review of compliance, an East-West confrontation was quite likely, one which could threaten the Belgrade meeting and even offer the possibility of a Soviet walkout (as feared by some Western and neutral countries). British Foreign Secretary David Owen posed the contradiction "between the legitimate expectation of [Western] public opinion [for review] on the one hand, and the potential danger of confrontation polemics on the other. . . ." He recommended that the contradiction be resolved by "adopting a balanced approach" between the two.

For Goldberg the balance had to be struck in the direction of a precise, judicious and judicial examination of compliance, letting the chips fall where they might. The finger of noncompliance had to be pointed at specific countries. Specific cases had to be mentioned and highlighted. It would have been an exercise in futility, according to Goldberg, were the Belgrade meeting to have consisted of a bland exchange of views similar to the blandness of vague charges at the UN. At the same time, in a break with past CSCE practices, the U.S. delegation decided to make available to the world media the text of speeches it was delivering at meetings, the position it was taking on various issues, and the arguments it was advancing.

The Goldberg perception did not coincide with the view of the U.S. diplomats who had played roles in the creation of the Helsinki Final Act. Springing from a tradition that had stressed the importance of a low profile, they resisted the revolutionary transformation. Goldberg's view, however, was supported by the U.S. Helsinki commission, which only further aggravated relations between the State Department and the commission.

The split in U.S. ranks mirrored a split in NATO. Goldberg

was scarcely the most popular man in NATO or with the neutrals and nonaligned. The fear of a Soviet walkout was strong, but it was Goldberg's opinion that the Soviet Union had too much at stake at Belgrade, including the personal reputation and commitment of Brezhnev, to withdraw. Of particular concern was the Goldberg determination to name names and cite specific cases. To him, that is what review of implementation meant. It took him weeks of negotiations with allies to get them to acquiesce to the United States pursuing this line.

Historic Meeting

The Belgrade meeting was unique, for it marked the first time in diplomatic history that the representatives of nearly all European states, the United States and Canada had gathered for the explicit purpose of reviewing compliance with an international document. A preparatory session to plan the agenda and the modalities started on June 15, 1977. Its progress was measured and deliberate as it had few prior guidelines and, more importantly, was certain to set basic precedents.

What emerged from the nine-week-long preparatory meeting was a key document, the Yellow Book, some nine pages of text, which comprised the organizational guidelines. The first and main phase of the Belgrade meeting would be devoted to reviewing implementation of the Final Act. The second phase would consider new proposals to further the CSCE process. The third phase would concentrate upon drafting a concluding document which would determine the date and place of the next review meeting. Agreement on the third phase was of critical importance because it committed the Helsinki signatories to a continuation of the Helsinki process, whatever happened in the substantive discussions.

Soviet Human Rights Violations

The Belgrade plenary opened on October 4, 1977. The review of implementation lasted eight weeks, during which the West, with the United States usually in the lead and Britain a close second, spelled out the lack of implementation by the U.S.S.R.

and Czechoslovakia of the Helsinki human rights provisions. Authorized to specify cases and names, the United States gave detailed attention to the Kremlin's repression of the Helsinki monitoring groups, mentioning a total of six names, including Orlov and Shcharansky, and the Prague crackdown on Charter 77. It cited other violations of Basket Three provisions— restrictions on emigration, on religious practices, on cultural rights and on the flow of information.

The Soviet Union rejected criticism of human rights compliance on the grounds that Principle VI of the Helsinki Final Act obliged signatories to "refrain from any intervention, direct or indirect, individual or collective, in the internal or external affairs falling under the domestic jurisdiction of another participating state. . . ." The argument arbitrarily redefined the text in a totally distorting manner. Principle VI specifically lists as prohibited acts "armed intervention or threat of such intervention" and "assistance to terrorist activities." Western criticism was in no way precluded. By Moscow's fiat, criticism was defined as intervention.

The Warsaw Pact delegates accused the United States of "poisoning the atmosphere" and of attempting to transform the meeting into a propaganda forum. But then their counteraction strategy changed. The U.S.S.R. proceeded to charge the United States with racism and other human rights violations, and social ills such as unemployment. The effect was to weaken the initial Soviet position that Principle VI precluded reference to specific countries. The West welcomed the change for it legitimized its view that inquiry into domestic practices was appropriate and indeed integral to the Helsinki process.

Still, the criticism never developed into a dialogue. "The U.S.S.R. and its allies refused to be drawn into any discussion of the merits of human rights cases brought up by the West," according to Fascell. Nor was dialogue possible in the second phase of the meeting dealing with new proposals. The U.S.S.R. advanced vague and broad proposals in the military security area that called for a treaty among CSCE signatories on no-first use of nuclear weapons and for "special joint consultations" on military issues. At the same time, the U.S.S.R. firmly opposed consideration of any new human rights proposals. Since the West was committed to "balance" between agreements on security and on human rights, deadlock was inevitable. Of the 100 new proposals that had been suggested, none was approved.

After a Christmas break, the Soviet delegation suddenly introduced, in virtual ultimatum form, a proposal for a concluding document that carried no reference to human rights. It was finally agreed to approve a short and terse statement asserting that the meeting had taken place, that a review of implementation had been held, that differences had been expressed, and that the next review meeting would be held in Madrid in the fall of 1980. In the meantime, the signatories agreed to three experts' meetings, including one in Hamburg, West Germany, dealing with science.

Belgrade Balance Sheet

In Goldberg's opening address at Belgrade, he spoke of the need of giving détente a "humanitarian face and a human measure." In that sense, Belgrade achieved a positive result. Largely due to Goldberg's insistence in the review meeting, human rights were placed in the central framework of multilateral diplomacy. Even the Yellow Book on the organization of the conference was given some authority for future meetings. Though the U.S.S.R. objected, it was agreed to have this "agenda" formula used in the planning of the next meeting.

Equally important was the acceptance of another review meeting two years after Belgrade. The U.S.S.R., increasingly suspicious of review meetings, proposed a four-year interval before the next meeting. But the West and the neutrals were insistent in demanding the shorter term lest the Helsinki process be seriously weakened.

If the U.S. leadership at Belgrade and its priority advocacy of human rights produced some positive developments, certain negative consequences were also to be noted, particularly with respect to the U.S. relationship with its NATO allies and the neutral and nonaligned group. Ambassador Sherer's wife Carroll disclosed shortly after the conclusion of the Belgrade meeting that the decision giving human rights high priority was taken with the understanding that considerations of a "possible fallout on other participants' expectations or on the future usefulness of the Helsinki document were secondary." Mrs. Sherer attributed the policy less to Goldberg than to the Carter White House which she blamed for deciding to use Belgrade "at the last minute" for its own "domestic political goals" and thereby furthering "the Administration's human rights campaign."

Los Angeles Times correspondent Don Cook reported at the time that the U.S. strategy caused disarray in NATO and nonaligned ranks and thereby played into the hands of the Russians. He reported that the United States had vetoed proposals of the neutral and nonaligned group and of the French because they were seen as too "mild" and the United States was insistent upon "a strong human rights formulation" in the concluding document. The result of the U.S. intransigence was to hand the U.S.S.R. a "victory." The headline of this article, written for *The Saturday Review,* was "Making America Look Foolish."

Ambassador Sherer in 1980 contended that at Belgrade NATO and the neutrals "viewed the [U.S.] confrontation strategy" as "a threat both to the CSCE process and to the health of political détente in Europe." He reported that the West Germans "felt undercut and betrayed" and that the neutrals were deprived of their "role of honest broker." In his view, the U.S. strategy at Belgrade, under Goldberg, was designed merely "to protect Carter's credibility on human rights." The result was alienation of our friends. This provided "a golden opportunity" to the U.S.S.R. "to drive wedges within the Western alliance and between it and the neutral states." Goldberg, in response to the Sherer charge, observed that "no ally in Belgrade has publicly criticized our delegation and its tactics as undermining political détente." And, he explained, the U.S. delegation "consulted our allies" throughout the conference, respected their criticisms, and at times "followed their advice, sometimes contrary to our best judgment."

Would another type of strategy have been more productive at

Belgrade? Had the United States been less confrontational, would it have produced better results? Congressman Fascell, after an examination of the record, concluded that "a softer Western approach at Belgrade would have meant a sterile meeting, full of self-serving, self-congratulatory rhetoric which mark East-West exchanges at other international forums."

An experts' meeting of distinguished scientists from the CSCE countries held in Hamburg in February 1980 would seem to validate the argument that a tough line on human rights need not be counterproductive. Despite scathing attacks by the United States, its allies and the neutrals upon the U.S.S.R. for its treatment of the great Soviet physicist Andrei Sakharov and the arrests, trials and convictions of other Soviet scientists, notably Orlov and Shcharansky, the Soviet delegation acquiesced in a final report of the scientists' meeting. The report made specific positive references to human rights in relations between states and in furthering cooperation between them.

The Soviet willingness to tolerate criticism and accept the human rights reference was probably due to its paramount interest in avoiding a break with Western scientists. That a scientists' conference could be held so soon after the invasion of Afghanistan and despite Western criticism of the Soviet aggression was itself sufficiently useful. There would be little point in jeopardizing the scientific contacts provided by such meetings. The crucial point is that when other Soviet interests are served, the Kremlin will tolerate being a target of criticism.

5

Madrid: Security
vs. Human Rights

The second CSCE review session was scheduled for Madrid on November 11, 1980, with preparatory sessions to begin two months earlier. While the prevailing hope since Belgrade was to avoid or prevent a repetition of the earlier superpower confrontation, tensions had not eased. The contrary was the case. Repression had intensified in the U.S.S.R., with the bulk of the Helsinki Watch Committee being brutally treated and Sakharov exiled to Gorki. Emigration of Jews, Germans and Armenians was greatly reduced. The status of human rights within the U.S.S.R. and Czechoslovakia could scarcely have been worse. If human rights were making considerable progress in Poland, that very progress aroused profound anxiety in the Kremlin, and Polish officials were being urged by Moscow to press for the liquidation of Solidarity and the uprooting of reformist trends.

The Soviet invasion of Afghanistan in December 1979 aroused special concern in the United States, where it was seen as violating both the spirit and letter of the Helsinki Final Act, even if Afghanistan was not a signatory. Certainly five of the ten basic principles of the Helsinki accord were either abridged or called into question, most notably those calling for "Refraining from the threat or use of force" and "Fulfillment in good faith of obligations under international law." The human rights principle was grossly challenged with the suppression of fundamental freedoms in Afghanistan. The U.S. response—to boycott the prestigious Olympics held in Moscow in the summer of 1980 and cut off the sale of grain and high-technology items to the U.S.S.R.—was indicative of the profound chill in East-West relations.

What America's posture should be toward Madrid, given the experience of Belgrade and the concern of other Western members and neutrals about confrontation threatening the Helsinki process, was the subject of intense controversy in Washington. An "executive summary" prepared by the State Department's Bureau of European Affairs (cited in an unpublished U.S. Helsinki commission staff memorandum) urged that the United States take primary account of the views of our NATO allies. They will "shrink" from a U.S. approach which seems to be "excessively confrontational" or which is designed "to appease domestic U.S. constituencies."

The commission staff memorandum urged a different course of action. It asked that a White House decision on the naming of names be reached quickly so that U.S. allies may be informed and Americans can then "seek to enlist their assistance and support for this tactic." If the United States fails to carry out a leadership role, "then no one will take the lead on human rights."

The White House tried to strike a balance between the State Department and the commission views. It went on record as seeking both a "candid review of progress in implementation of the Final Act" and the consideration of new proposals, including a French proposal for a CSCE-sponsored Conference on Disarmament in Europe.

Diplomat's Diplomat

Juxtaposing and, indeed, linking security concerns with human rights objectives was by no means a simple task. And yet this aim was essential, indeed indispensable, if the weaknesses of the Belgrade meeting were not to be repeated. Could the United States exercise leadership and promote human rights vigorously and, at the same time, encourage and permit Western Europe to play far more than a subordinate role?

The circle would be squared by the choice made to head the U.S. delegation under both Presidents Carter and Reagan. Max M. Kampelman, a prominent attorney who had once served as the principal aide of Senator Hubert Humphrey, was selected by Carter as the operating head of the U.S. delegation, with former Attorney General Griffin Bell as the official leader. Bell spent relatively little time in Madrid. Later, with Reagan in the White House, Kampelman, a Democrat, was asked to continue and, indeed, lead the U.S. delegation. It was a most unusual decision. He was one of very few Carter appointees who was asked to continue in his post. What made the Reagan decision particularly intriguing was the fact that, as a candidate, Reagan had expressed doubts about the value of U.S. participation in the Madrid proceedings. Reagan's choice testified to a changed outlook on the Madrid meeting and a realization of its value. And it also indicated that Kampelman had displayed talents as a good articulator and implementer of U.S. policy and an effective negotiator who worked unusually well with both the NATO partners and the neutrals.

The U.S. delegation under Kampelman would give human rights the highest priority. Before doing so, it had to win a decisive procedural battle. At the preparatory meetings, the U.S.S.R. engaged in a major filibustering maneuver designed to limit the compliance review to only two and one-half days or, at most, one or two weeks. The review of implementation was, of course, central to American strategy. At Belgrade it had run some nine weeks as part of the Yellow Book. The U.S.S.R. now rejected the Yellow Book as a guideline and tried to have the regular session concentrate on new proposals. The West, under U.S. leadership, fought for an unlimited period of compliance review.

A second Soviet maneuver focused upon the question of the time and place of the subsequent review meeting. Moscow sought to leave the question up in the air by deliberately withholding assent. The device was aimed at keeping review meetings hostage to a more accommodating conduct by the West.

The stonewalling tactics were deliberate, designed to exploit and widen differences between the allies. The Kremlin was keenly aware of the powerful interest in détente among both European NATO members and neutrals. Their fears could be played upon to reduce the amount of time devoted to review of implementation. With everyone remembering the disarray in Western ranks at Belgrade, the filibuster posed a real challenge.

At midnight November 11, the date of the scheduled opening of the Madrid conference, the agenda was still up in the air and the clock was stopped. The key issue revolved around the question of whether the U.S.S.R. was prepared to bury the Helsinki accord—and détente as well. Some West Europeans, particularly among the neutrals, were nervous about the delicate tightrope maneuvers. The U.S. strategy was guided by the conviction that the U.S.S.R. was not prepared to junk the Helsinki agreement. While the deadlock continued, a high Italian official visited Soviet Foreign Minister Gromyko in Moscow and bitterly complained about the filibuster in Madrid. Gromyko told him that the Madrid conference was certain to be held. When this was reported to the NATO caucus in Madrid, tension diminished.

Indeed, Soviet strategy was largely bluff. A top-ranking Soviet official later confided to an American delegate that "we have instructions to work closely with you." Clearly, détente was not to be prematurely discarded. But the strategy of stonewalling and brinksmanship was based upon a serious miscalculation. Yuri Dubinin, the Soviet ambassador to Spain and the second-ranking official in the delegation at Madrid, privately disclosed to Warsaw Pact colleagues that the Kremlin had not expected either the tough adamancy of the Americans or the tightness in NATO ranks. Dubinin himself was gratified by the outcome, according to East European sources. He told them that had the stonewalling pushed the conference over the brink, he would have lost his job.

Soviet Stake in Madrid Review

The Soviet Union was pursuing a major foreign policy objective at Madrid. This was the fundamental difference between the Belgrade and Madrid review conferences, and it provided the

West, particularly the United States, with both leverage and a critical bargaining chip. Brezhnev had spoken of the Soviet objective in a rare interview in *Pravda* marking the fifth anniversary of the Helsinki Final Act. In the interview, Brezhnev noted that the forthcoming review meeting must lead to "important" results, including specifically the convening of a conference on military détente and disarmament.

The fact that France shared somewhat similar objectives was a major asset for the U.S.S.R. As early as May 1978, France had submitted a memorandum to CSCE members calling for a two-stage conference on disarmament. In the first stage, the conference would focus on confidence-building measures, amplifying upon and extending those on prior notification of military maneuvers and exchange of observers, as stipulated in the Helsinki Final Act. The second stage would concentrate on an examination of measures for the actual limitation and reduction of conventional weapons and forces. To avoid both premature failure and the abuse of the forum for purely propaganda purposes, France emphasized that the second stage should be called only "when substantial results, regarded as satisfactory by all participants, have already been achieved."

When the French plan was first introduced, the United States refused to discuss it. Not only was there concern about the abuse of a CSCE forum; there was deep anxiety that human rights would be sacrificed to security concerns. President Carter, in his own Helsinki anniversary speech on July 29, 1980, emphasized that Helsinki "should not become significantly an arms control forum."

The French view ultimately prevailed within NATO, although with important changes that eased the fears of France's principal allies. On December 13–14, 1979, the NATO foreign ministers, meeting in Brussels, Belgium, accepted the basic features of the French proposal as "a useful concept." They agreed to work at Madrid toward this objective, provided it was interrelated with the CSCE process and was "part of a balanced outcome." The key word was "balanced." It meant that approval of a two-stage disarmament conference would require Soviet concessions in the human rights field. Equally important was how the mandate would be described. A meeting on confidence-building must deal with "measures" that are "militarily significant," "verifiable" and "applicable to the entire continent of Europe." The subsequent NATO foreign ministers' meeting in Ankara, Turkey, in June 1980 defined "the entire continent of Europe" as including "the whole of the European part of the Soviet Union" bounded by the Ural mountains.

Europe's Boundaries Redefined

The Helsinki Final Act had envisaged Europe's eastern boundary as extending only 250 kilometers (150 miles) into the Soviet Union. The Soviet Urals reach almost 10 times that distance. A modification of the Final Act would therefore be required, even though the Urals as a boundary line seem both reasonable and appropriate for a body designated a "Conference on Security and Cooperation in *Europe*" (emphasis added).

The Kremlin could not but view the French proposal with considerable interest in light of the scheduled installation of U.S. cruise and Pershing II missiles in Western Europe. Indeed the Soviets were prepared to shelve a more tendentious 1979 Warsaw Pact proposal for a conference on arms reduction in favor of the French one. Since the French had placed stress on confidence-building measures that would extend to the Urals, Brezhnev went out of his way in a major policy address to the 26th Congress of the Soviet Communist party in February 1981 to accept publicly the new demarcation, provided the West made a geographical concession.[1]

To win support for the disarmament conference, the head of the Soviet delegation, Leonid F. Ilyichev, the deputy foreign minister, appeared to be hinting at a quid pro quo in human rights in his opening statement at Madrid. The Soviet delegation, he said, was prepared to consider "in a businesslike way" three types of problems: "easing of conditions for the reunion of families" and for the "consummation of marriages between citizens of different states"; and measures for "the development of useful contacts in the fields of culture, information, education, and science."

What the Soviet Union had not anticipated was the tough Western stand which forced the Soviet hand. A last-minute proposal advanced by the neutrals, which set a six-week period for review of implementation and which carried a "take-it-or-leave-it" ultimatum, finally won Soviet approval.

A priority objective of the United States had been achieved. There would now be adequate time for a line-by-line review of the Final Act. Implementation of Principle VII would be thoroughly examined. Every key item in Basket Three—human contacts, freedom of movement and information, reunification of families, and cultural relations—was covered by the West in considerable detail.

Sixty-five cases were specifically discussed during the initial review session as compared with but six at Belgrade. (By 1983, the number of cases raised ran to 121.) The plight of the Helsinki monitors—the harassments, trials, convictions and exiles—was spelled out. The record of repression was revealing: of 71 original members of the Helsinki monitoring groups, 24 had been tried and convicted (19 of whom were serving a total of 156 years of forced labor and exile), 11 more were under arrest, 9 were serving previously imposed jail sentences, 7 were encouraged to emigrate and 2 were stripped of their citizenship while traveling abroad. Similarly, the Soviet Jewish torment was disclosed in considerable detail: the profound 90 percent cutback in emigration; the psychological distress of the refuseniks who were denied exit visas; the gutting of Jewish cultural institutions and rights; and the mounting of a vast anti-Semitic propaganda campaign.

The second essential aim intrinsic to the Helsinki process was also won when the U.S.S.R. agreed that the Madrid participants would set the time and place of the next review meeting, thereby keeping the Helsinki process in motion. Both Rumania and Belgium were bidding for the site in their respective capitals. But it was clear, early on, that a variety of considerations would dictate the choice of a neutral site. (Vienna, Austria, was ultimately chosen as the site of the 1986 meeting.)

Both on human rights and on the crucial issue of NATO unity, Kampelman proved an effective spokesman for the Administration and an extraordinarily talented negotiator. NATO caucuses were held two to three times a week, and the Americans sought to encourage others to take the initiative and even assume leadership on various issues. Kampelman avoided strong-arm and overbearing techniques. Even if uniformity of opinion was precluded by the separate interests of the parties, diverse perceptions were subordinated to a common approach. Kampelman would use a musical metaphor to make his point. "In an orchestra," he told his colleagues, "there is need for a drummer as well as a harpist; what is most important is that we play music together."

There was almost universal support for the American position on human rights, even to the extent that a number of allies decided to intervene on this issue, in striking contrast to the policy of total silence that had prevailed at Belgrade. Solidarity was also maintained on the Afghanistan issue. Virtually every Western and neutral delegation, 26 in all, rose to brand the Soviet military invasion as a violation of key principles of the Helsinki accord. When Ilyichev protested that the Western criticism constituted intervention in internal affairs, he evoked smiles and suppressed laughter in Western ranks.

Western unity permitted the United States' confrontational challenge to range over a broad philosophical area. The Western system of values with its emphasis upon the individual was contrasted with the Soviet system of collective values: "collective values bring with them suppression of the individual," Kampelman noted, thereby depriving the latter of his freedom explicitly provided by the Helsinki Final Act. Illustrations were abundant: the dismaying internal exile of Sakharov, the scandalous trials of the Helsinki monitoring leaders, the sudden arrest on the eve of the Madrid conference of Jewish intellectual and refusenik Viktor Brailovsky.

In cultivating NATO, the United States also pursued a related objective: the enlargement of NATO by the addition of Spain. Its delegates were invited to sit in on NATO caucus meetings and to participate as an active member of the Western bloc. If not every West European country was as anxious to bring Spain into the alliance, this scarcely hindered the U.S. delegation from being especially attentive to Spain's role and status. The effect was to align Spain more closely with the West. Diplomacy was by no means shunted aside in the interests of human rights ideology or propaganda.

Solidarity's Eclipse

Allied unity permitted a common course to be adopted with respect to the imposition of martial law in Poland on December 13, 1981, and the suppression of Solidarity and human rights in that country. It was made clear to the U.S.S.R. and Poland that "business as usual" could no longer be followed, and further negotiations on a series of proposals advanced by the neutrals were brought to a halt.

At the behest of the allies, still anxious and determined to maintain the framework of the Helsinki accord, the United States agreed to the resumption of the Madrid meeting on February 9, after the Christmas recess, with the proviso that there would be no negotiations.

Just prior to February 9, Deputy Foreign Minister Jozef Wiejacz of Poland, whose representative was to serve as chairman of the resumed session, warned: "We shall not take part in conferences in which Poland would be made to stand in the dock." But Poland was obliged to do just that. Several Western foreign ministers joined Secretary of State Alexander M. Haig Jr. on February 9 in a powerful verbal assault on Poland and the U.S.S.R. When the Poles sought to halt other Western foreign ministers from speaking through a series of procedural maneuvers, they provoked a profoundly negative reaction, further solidifying allied ranks and angering the neutrals. The Austrian foreign minister sharply criticized "those who prevent speakers from speaking." Even the Finnish delegate observed that Soviet strategy was counterproductive. It was decided to bring a halt to the session and, in opposition to Soviet objectives for further discussions, the allies joined in a veritable silent sit-down strike. The adamancy of the allies compelled an adjournment of the session on March 12.

When it became clear later in 1982 that West European countries were anxious to return to Madrid to discuss détente and security issues, further coordination of the NATO position became necessary. Since the U.S. opposition to Polish military rule was especially firm, the West Europeans felt prompted to seek the resumption of the Madrid session only after agreement was reached on a common human rights position. Denmark proposed that NATO press for 14 human rights amendments, including recognition of trade unions, the right to strike, and the end of jamming of Western broadcasts. With an eye to winning U.S. approval for a resumption of the Madrid conference, NATO accepted the proposal. What was evident was the continuing search for a common line that would take account of conflicting interests. It was a testimonial to U.S. statesmanship that, at least in Madrid, this effort proved successful.

In September, after nearly three years of almost endless debate and interminable wrangling, the Madrid review session ended with the Helsinki process given a modest boost forward. The Madrid conference may have surpassed by far all previous talkfests in the decade-old history of CSCE, but it proved significantly more successful than the Belgrade meeting where no proposals had been accepted and the participants simply had agreed to disagree.

Among the human rights proposals initially advanced by the neutrals and nonaligned and approved at Madrid were a commitment to combat terrorism and a pledge to assure some progress with respect to religious freedom. A consensus decision was also reached providing for "the right of workers freely to establish and join trade unions." The implication for Poland especially, and for the other Warsaw Pact countries, was self-evident. The Helsinki signatories agreed to allow their nationals access to foreign missions and gave foreign journalists the right "to establish and maintain personal contacts and communication with their sources." Agreement was also reached on holding a conference of experts on human rights.

1986 Bern Conference

Especially significant was a decision to hold a "human contacts" meeting in Bern, Switzerland, in April 1986. Such a meeting is certain to focus upon the issue of reunification of families and Soviet violations of the Helsinki provisions. In the face of strong Soviet resistance to this proposal, which had initially been advanced by the United States and Canada (and backed by NATO), the neutral and nonaligned group chose not to press for such a meeting. But the West, under U.S. leadership, was determined not to capitulate on this critical issue which went to the very heart of the cardinal right to emigrate.

The deadlock was broken when Spanish Socialist Prime Minister Felipe González on June 17, 1983, personally appealed to the participants to agree to hold the human contacts conference. He sought to sweeten his recommendation by urging that the West drop its proposal that would strike at radio jamming by requiring the "free flow" of information over international broadcasts. In view of the modest progress registered in the human rights area, the West was willing to drop its anti-jamming demand just as it had earlier decided not to press for the rest of the 14-point package of February 1982. Meanwhile, the two principal Soviet delegates flew to Moscow to ascertain whether their stonewalling should be continued. After returning to Madrid, Deputy Foreign Minister Anatoly Kovalev announced at a closed session on July 1 that "the Soviet delegation is ready to act within the framework of the initiative of the Spanish government."

Soviet reluctance to irritate the host country, whose Socialist prime minister it was seeking to cultivate on security issues, was certainly a factor in Moscow's decision. Far more important, however, was its determination to gain agreement on the conference on confidence-building measures, which it had so desperately sought since the beginning of the Madrid session and which hinged on its acquiescence to the Spanish initiative. Allied firmness on the human contacts question, Moscow recognized, could not be budged. Continuation of the deadlock would jeopardize its major aspiration.

Stockholm Conference

Agreement on a conference on confidence-building measures was, of course, the principal decision made in Madrid. Western

Europe was interested in such a conference in the hope that additional ways would be devised there to ward off surprise attack. In addition, the proposed conference would be welcomed by the growing peace movement in the West. The neutrals and nonaligned countries regarded the conference idea as a crucial first step for reviving the earlier détente atmosphere.

Moscow failed, however, in its anxious endeavor to have the conference held *prior* to NATO's planned installation of U.S. cruise and Pershing II missiles in Western Europe, scheduled for December 1983. Under the Madrid compromise arrangement, the conference was scheduled to be held in Stockholm, Sweden, in January 1984.

The numerous adjustments worked into the final document enabled the Helsinki process, despite the delays and frustrations, to move forward. Some of the participants began speaking about a "spirit of Madrid" that might breathe life into détente. The fact that Moscow suddenly decided in mid-June to allow some 15 Russian Pentecostals from Siberia, who had been housed in the U.S. embassy for several years, to emigrate to Israel contributed to the "spirit."

Still, excessive enthusiasm would be unwarranted. Emigration of Jews, Germans and Armenians is at a standstill. Orlov and Shcharansky languish in forced-labor camps. Anti-Semitism is once again raising its ugly head. And abridgment of the Helsinki accord's freedom and rights—including the key "right of the individual to know and act upon his rights"—still prevails in the U.S.S.R. and elsewhere in Eastern Europe.

---

[1]At first the Soviets wanted the West to agree to notify the East in advance of any military maneuvers held in the eastern half of the United States and Canada. When the West refused, they insisted that, at a minimum, the West notify them of maneuvers extending deep into the Atlantic. Those demands were likewise rejected. The Soviets ultimately agreed to a nonaligned compromise providing for advance notification of air, naval and military maneuvers in the seas adjoining the European continent.

6

The Value of the
Helsinki Process

In the 10 years since CSCE was created, a radical transformation has taken place in how the United States views the
conference. CSCE, in the words of Under Secretary of State
Lawrence S. Eagleburger, is "terribly valuable to the whole
process of American foreign policy." It "gives us a forum that the
Soviets simply cannot ignore, nor can the people of the world
ignore, to remind the world of their failure to meet their
commitments under the Helsinki Final Act." Second, the Helsinki process "gives us a place in a forum which discusses
European issues" and, were the United States not there, "what
you [would] have . . . is the Soviet Union talking to Europeans
about European problems, where[as] I think it is clear that
European issues are in fact American issues as well."

Considerable public attention has focused on human rights.
Among the nongovernmental organizations that have played a
major role are the U.S. Helsinki Watch Committee, Amnesty
International, Freedom House, the International League for
Human Rights, and the World Conference on Soviet Jewry.
Belgrade and especially Madrid resounded with the recitation of

Soviet violations of the Final Act. This inevitably raises the question whether any human rights benefits have resulted. Certainly prior to Belgrade, to counter the expected criticism at that forum, the U.S.S.R. permitted a greater flow of emigration of both Jews and Germans, and it hesitated to place several arrested Helsinki monitors on trial, most notably Shcharansky.

The Soviet Union, however, did not hesitate to abridge Helsinki human rights provisions before and during the Madrid conference. In fact the Soviet crackdown on human rights was at its most intense during the Madrid session. Over 300 were arrested for one or another human rights activities, the Helsinki monitoring committees were totally silenced, and emigration of Jews and Germans was reduced to a trickle. The Kremlin's top career secret police official, writing in the principal party journal *Kommunist* in September 1981, took pride in the suppression of dissent. Referring to the Helsinki monitors as "so-called defenders of human rights," he denounced them as "anti-Socialist elements" who either were Western "agents" striving for subversion of Soviet society or were exploited by the West. A month later, the chief Soviet delegate at Madrid condemned the Western supporters of the monitors for engaging in "interference" in Soviet "internal affairs" through "demagogy and empty verbiage aimed at misleading people."

Nonetheless, there have been instances when some of the more flagrant forms of Soviet human rights abuse have been modified. A particularly unusual example was provided by a Jewish "prisoner of conscience," Iosif Mendelevich, a deeply religious person, who had started a hunger strike in his forced labor camp in November 1980. He was approached by the camp administrator, who sought to discourage him from the strike. Mendelevich told the administrator that he, as a prisoner, was "an unimportant person to Soviet power." The administrator's response, as revealed by Mendelevich, was instructive: "You are wrong because you are not alone. There is a Madrid conference at the present time, and many things have happened in the world which the Soviets have to take into account." Several months later Mendelevich was released, one year before the end of a 12-year sentence. Upon arriving in Israel, in February 1981, he disclosed the details of the episode.

The case of Sakharov's hunger strike is a second example. The fiancée of his adopted son (the young man was the son of Sakharov's second wife, Elena Bonner) had been repeatedly refused an exit visa to join her husband-to-be, who had previously emigrated and was living in the Boston area. Sakharov, in launching his hunger strike in 1981, sent a plea to the Madrid meeting asking that the matter be raised as a violation of Helsinki's Basket Three. A copy was urgently forwarded to Ambassador Kampelman. The potential impact upon the Madrid discussions must have played some part in the Kremlin decision to allow the fiancée to emigrate.

'Don't Abandon Us'

From the point of view of Soviet activists and dissenters, the Helsinki Final Act has served as the principal banner to which they can cling and Madrid was the sounding board for their hopes and aspirations. A stream of appeals and petitions flowed to Madrid with the thought that their conditions might ease or even, conceivably, that they might be granted their requests. Activists do not perceive the forum of Helsinki as worsening their plight; instead, they see it, in most cases, as relieving more extreme forms of repression and as the indispensable means for maintaining hope and sustaining morale.

Congressman Elliott H. Levitas (D-Ga.), after an official visit to the U.S.S.R. in January 1982, reported that Soviet activists with whom he had met considered the Madrid meeting as "vital for their security and well-being." It was a typical view given to prominent Western visitors. In January 1983, when a delegation of the U.S. Helsinki commission traveled to the Soviet Union, they were told by dissenters and activists, "don't abandon us in Madrid."

Another example of a positive, if delayed, response came on the issue of Soviet anti-Semitism. The Soviet delegation at the Madrid meeting was particularly stung by charges made by representatives of West European countries about anti-Jewish practices in the U.S.S.R. No doubt such accusations aroused anxiety that the Soviet Union could be associated with the hated philosophy of Nazism. In late November 1980 several Western delegates had raised the issue, but none as forcefully as the Belgian representative, René Panis. In a Basket Three commission meeting, he provided various illustrations of the Kremlin's "intensified anti-Semitism" which, he said, revealed a "rising mercury level in that horrible barometer" of hate. Observers recall that the Soviet delegate, in responding, was ashen-faced and shaking as he waved a copy of the Soviet constitution, which he said banned anti-Semitism. This was followed by a shouted non sequitur to the effect that since it was banned by statute, anti-Semitism "never existed and never will exist in Soviet society."

A more vigorous and powerful response came from a totally unexpected source three months later. Brezhnev, in the course of a five-hour policy address to the 26th Congress of the Soviet Communist party, specifically denounced anti-Semitism as a "nationalist aberration" that is "alien to the nature of socialism." The condemnation was unique in the annals of party history. At no party Congress since 1898 has the party leader singled out anti-Semitism for criticism in a policy speech. The Brezhnev condemnation was the first by a high Communist official since 1965, when Prime Minister Kosygin castigated anti-Semitism in a speech published in *Pravda*. Analysts found that after the Brezhnev speech, some of the more vulgar and obscene forms of Soviet anti-Semitism in the Soviet media were either eliminated or modified.

Thus the Helsinki process communicates a message at two levels to the Soviet Union. On one level it addresses the activists, dissidents, and the concentric circles who constitute their friends or who may be responsive to the canons of international law or the moral foundations of civilized society. On the second level it addresses the Soviet government. "One of our primary purposes," said Kampelman in a recent talk to U.S. diplomats in Europe, "is to send a continuing and consistent message which clearly communicates to Soviet authorities . . . our deep and specific concerns about their behavior. . . ." He is keenly aware of the fact

Madrid, July 1983: Ambassador Max Kampelman (left) and U.S. Ambassador to Spain Terence Todman confer on the wording of a compromise document concluding the Madrid review meeting.

that his speeches are forwarded to Moscow immediately after sessions.

To reinforce the seriousness with which the United States is committed to human rights issues, Kampelman communicated with his Soviet counterpart in Madrid by letter or in private meetings and raised specific cases or issues. The private dialogues were extensive and somewhat extraordinary. By July 1983, Kampelman had held some 300 hours of off-the-record discussions with the Soviet Ambassador, whether Ilyichev or his successor, Kovalev. The dialogues were not restricted to human rights issues. They ranged over the entire area of American concerns as they relate to the U.S.S.R.

The nonpublic dialogue within the Madrid framework was a remarkably useful means for maintaining contact and communicating with the U.S.S.R. Indeed, until the start of the Geneva talks on intermediate-range nuclear weapons late in 1982,

Madrid was the only site—beyond traditional diplomatic channels—of an ongoing dialogue with the Soviets. During the course of these private meetings, a constant flow of signals was transmitted. The United States might indicate a special interest in a particular dissident or an unpublicized way of resolving a foreign policy issue. The U.S.S.R. also used the occasion to make its concerns felt. The communication of a message need not produce immediate results. But its constant repetition over a period of time can prove and, indeed, has in the past at times proved effective. Quiet diplomacy can reinforce the public outcry in the human rights field, especially over the long run. It is for that reason that Kampelman has pleaded for patience in dealing with the Russians.

Communications Channel with Eastern Europe

The Soviet Union is not the only focal point of America's human rights concerns. America's involvement in the Helsinki process enables it to affect attitudes, especially in the human rights field, in various countries in Eastern Europe aside from the U.S.S.R. For several Communist countries, the Helsinki process has provided and continues to provide a multilateral framework within which bilateral discussions are both tolerated and acceptable. Channels outside the Helsinki framework are quite limited, even with the presence of embassies or through UN organs. Prior to review sessions, a dialogue is conducted with each of the Communist governments as American delegations are sent to various capitals to take soundings on positions concerning key upcoming issues and the degree of implementation of Helsinki's provisions. During the review meetings in Madrid, the dialogue continued, although it was limited by the discipline maintained within the Warsaw Pact structure by Soviet authority.

Progress Report

The human rights provisions of the Helsinki Final Act have exerted a significant liberalizing impact upon a number of East European countries, a crucial fact that appears to have gone unnoticed in the West. A report issued in June 1981 by President

Reagan to the Helsinki commission illuminates the broad range of responses in Eastern Europe—especially in the area of freer movement of people. Although the situation in Poland has worsened, the improvements in other countries noted in that report still obtain.

While Hungary for some time had permitted emigration to expedite reunion of families, the situation also improved in Bulgaria, Czechoslovakia and East Germany. Similarly, travel to these countries by Western citizens, especially for family visits, was eased. Visas for those involved in binational marriage became feasible. Even Czechoslovakia, which mimics Soviet conduct in most human rights matters, was reported to have a "good record" in resolving family reunion cases with the United States. The same applied to visitation cases.

Hungary's record was especially good, with the number of family visits to the United States running into the thousands and almost no denial of visas to Americans seeking to visit family members in Hungary, according to the President's report. Particularly impressive was the temporary turnabout in Poland's conduct following the Solidarity movement's success and the ouster of the Edward Gierek regime in September 1980. On the eve of the Madrid meeting, the Warsaw government, in what was termed by the United States "a major positive development," resolved some 550 outstanding cases of Polish citizens seeking to emigrate to the United States. Significant differences, however, prevailed with regard to travel rights for personal or professional reasons, which are specified in the Final Act. Hungary and Poland (for a brief time) maintained a liberal travel policy while the others followed the Soviet practice of applying tight control on tourist travel by their citizens. Visas were especially eased for those seeking to marry a national from another country or to join a spouse who was a foreign national. Except for Rumania and the U.S.S.R., most abided by the obligations in respect to binational marriages involving Americans.

Basket Three emphasized, besides emigration and travel, the freer movement of ideas. In the category of dissemination of information, only Poland had taken "serious steps forward in terms of fuller implementation of the provisions of the Helsinki Final Act," the 1981 U.S. report noted. Elsewhere, the pattern was quite restrictive, especially with regard to Western publications, books and films. While much of Eastern Europe followed the Soviet pattern of jamming Western radio broadcasts, although by no means as intensively, Hungary, Rumania and East Germany did not. Working conditions for journalists were quite good in Poland before martial law was imposed in December 1981, and, to a lesser extent, in Hungary and Bulgaria. Elsewhere the restrictive Soviet model prevailed.

Visits by orchestras, artists, theatrical companies, exhibits and academic specialists, along with exchange programs involving scholars, students and scientific researchers, were widespread by-products of the Helsinki Final Act, and involved the Soviet Union's Warsaw Pact allies. The exchange programs, particularly, were perceived as having been fruitful in expanding horizons and extending the flow of ideas. According to a Ford Foundation specialist who had been involved in these exchange programs sanctioned by the Helsinki Final Act, they had "a significant impact on dissent in Eastern Europe" in that they helped "introduce alternative ideas and ways of looking at things which would not otherwise be permitted."

Fellowships for study in the United States and elsewhere in the West, granted by leading academic institutions, were not without a critical effect. Among Polish winners, not surprisingly, several became prominent lecturers in the "Flying University" of the Polish renaissance associated with Solidarity, or followed other independent intellectual pursuits. Fellowship winners and alumni of exchange programs frequently could be found among independent thinkers in Poland, Hungary, Czechoslovakia, Rumania and East Germany. To what extent the exchange programs affected the initial Solidarity movement in Poland cannot, of course, be determined with any degree of accuracy. But that a definite relationship existed between the reform movement and Poland's participation in the Helsinki process is undoubted. One of the principal demands of Solidarity, as with KOR, was the government's full adherence to the Helsinki Final Act.

Western Unity and U.S. Security

Besides being a forum for human rights, the Madrid review, as Eagleburger noted, served as a forum to air U.S. security concerns in Europe. It is, of course, true that the United States was obliged to accommodate itself to European views concerning a conference on confidence-building measures and disarmament, but, at the same time, it has exerted influence on the kind of conference which would be acceptable, and it has succeeded in tying that conference to human rights progress. The responsiveness of the United States to its NATO allies and to the neutrals has been noteworthy and has put Moscow in the position of having to cope with a united Western position.

Eagleburger, in testimony at a CSCE hearing, sharply rejected the viewpoint that the Helsinki process be "chucked in" because significant progress has not been made in human rights and because a stalemate prevailed on central issues, including security. In his view, the Helsinki review process "is an important element of our foreign policy, and one that keeps the pressure on the other side, and one that is 100 percent an advantage to the United States and to the West."

In contrast to 1974 when it had basked in the glow of Helsinki, Moscow no longer extends hosannas to Helsinki. A stunning, if almost unnoticed, downplaying has taken place in official statements and in the media. Only intermittently do leading Soviet officials refer to the Helsinki accord and then, usually, in a defensive manner.

Soviet Doublespeak

The principles of Basket One, as noted earlier, were arbitrarily redefined by the Soviets so as to preclude the raising of human rights issues on grounds that it constitutes intervention in the internal affairs of states. The question of "reunification of families" was the heart of the fundamental aspiration for "freer movement of peoples." But "family" is now officially redefined by a high Soviet official to include "only husbands, wives, and their unmarried children." Thus, the purpose of the Final Act to ease emigration procedures is inverted so as to limit emigration.

Refusals of visas on grounds of "insufficient closeness of relatives" have become quite common.

Equally outrageous is the Soviet use of the International Covenant on Civil and Political Rights to negate the application of the Helsinki Final Act. Deputy Minister of Interior Boris Shumilin declared: "Restrictions that we sometimes impose proceed directly from the clauses of the [International] Covenant on Civil and Political Rights." Shumilin failed to note that such "restrictions" are to be applied only as they are "provided by law." Indeed, the thrust of the right-to-leave clause in the covenant is in the direction of greater freedom of movement.

"National security" became the principal reason given for refusing exit visas. A survey conducted among refusenik families indicated that three quarters of the refusals were based on "security." In most cases, however, the refused applicant either never had access to "state secrets" or had ceased his employment long before he made application to leave. Caprice of an all-embracing character exists in Soviet decisionmaking in this field. With no published law covering such restrictions, the applicant is deprived of a fundamental right "to know his rights." The Soviet Union's version of George Orwell's novel *1984* was detailed on November 9, 1976, by *Tass* and published the next day in *Izvestiya:* ". . . The secrets of a state are always its exclusive property. That is why it is an internal question for the Soviet Union to decide which specific works or information are to be considered secret . . . ." In this way, even the restrictive provision of the right-to-leave clause in the International Covenant on Civil and Political Rights is emptied of meaning. The monumental Kremlin effort to manipulate and distort the language of the Final Act only testifies to the significance of the Helsinki accord, not its inadequacy.

At the Madrid review, when individual human rights cases were documented by Western delegates, Soviet spokesmen either failed to respond or responded briefly with generalized comments rejecting the documentation as "misleading" or "subject to considerable doubt." So long as a possibility existed for reaching an agreement on a conference dealing with confidence-building measures, they were reluctant to jeopardize it with verbal violence.

Strikingly, the Soviet delegation avoided any intimation of a walkout or threat of a walkout and expressed interest in "a consistent continuation" of the Helsinki process. Two key considerations guided this decision. First was Brezhnev's personal involvement. The Final Act was said to have constituted "a brilliant success" for Brezhnev's personal diplomacy. Whether Brezhnev's death and his replacement by Yuri V. Andropov will bring about a change in posture cannot be determined. Initially Andropov failed to refer to the Helsinki process even though in one of his first addresses he spoke exultantly about détente and its value to Soviet foreign policy. The Helsinki Final Act was and is the major institutional expression of détente, and it appeared curious that Andropov would choose not to mention it. More recently, he has addressed himself to the Helsinki process in a brief and formal manner without the enthusiasm which characterized Brezhnev's approach. On the other hand, it did not go unnoticed that his son was assigned to the Soviet delegation to the Madrid review conference when it resumed in November 1982. And while he ranked fifth in the delegation, he was assigned the task of making several important statements.

The second and more important motivation for rejecting a walkout remained hard policy interests. The Helsinki accord, from the beginning, was seen as a forum for exploiting differences between Washington and its NATO allies. Emphasis has been placed repeatedly, and all the more so now, on disarmament and on the benefits to Western Europe of trade with the U.S.S.R.

To the extent that the Kremlin can expect to use the Helsinki process to generate or aggravate tensions between the United States and Western Europe, it will continue to find future review meetings valuable. Besides, it would damage the Soviet image among the neutrals and nonaligned, as well as among its supporters in Western Europe, were it to attempt to distance itself from the Helsinki accord. The test inevitably rests with American diplomacy.

The value placed upon the Madrid meeting was underscored

by President Reagan in a formal statement on July 15, 1983, which approved the concluding compromise document. He noted that the Madrid agreement, together with the Helsinki accord, "sets forth a clear code of conduct for all 35 states—a set of standards to which we and the other Atlantic democracies will continue to hold those who will have pledged their word at Madrid." After calling attention to the "gradual and hard-won" results achieved at the Madrid conference, President Reagan observed that there remains the critical "challenge" of ensuring that the "good words are transformed into good deeds." He added: "Giving substance to the promises of Madrid and Helsinki will remain one of our prime objectives."

The human rights advances, even if limited, were not the only positive consequence of the Madrid meeting. The agreements reached and the trade-offs made set the stage for a broader diplomatic purpose—high-level summitry between the United States and the Soviet Union that could focus on a wide range of concerns and tensions. President Reagan alluded to this outcome when he commented that the agreement might serve the U.S. "objective of a more stable and constructive relationship with the Soviet Union." The initial stage of the summitry was a meeting of Secretary of State George P. Shultz with Soviet Foreign Minister Gromyko on the occasion of the signing of the Madrid accord in September 1983. Projected as a possible second stage was a meeting between President Reagan and Soviet President Andropov, the first between the two leaders.

The encouraging, if small, steps toward a summit were abruptly suspended by the Soviet shooting down of a South Korean commercial airliner on September 1, 1983, killing 269 people. The brutal and callous act led to a sharp confrontation at Madrid between Shultz and Gromyko in which the United States charged that the Kremlin placed a far lower priority upon human rights than upon security. It was the theme that had characterized Madrid even as it was central to all CSCE discussions since its birth a decade ago. Madrid, at the end, became the ultimate forum for driving home the fundamental U.S. posture on human rights. The Helsinki process clearly has become an integral and crucial element in American diplomacy.

Talking It Over

A Note for Students and Discussion Groups

This issue of the HEADLINE SERIES, like its predecessors, is published for every serious reader, specialized or not, who takes an interest in the subject. Many of our readers will be in classrooms, seminars or community discussion groups. Particularly with them in mind, we present below some discussion questions—suggested as a starting point only—and references for further reading.

Discussion Questions

Why and how did the CSCE come into existence? What was its relationship to détente? In what way could it be said that the U.S.S.R. was the prime mover in its creation? Why was the Soviet Union prompted to play such a role?

Explain in general terms the Helsinki Final Act. To what extent could it be said to be a trade-off between security considerations of the East and human rights aims of the West? Principle VII dealing with human rights has been characterized as a milestone in international diplomacy. Why?

Compare the Madrid review meeting with Belgrade. To what extent and why did Madrid show progress with respect to the Helsinki process? How did "balance" between the "baskets" of the Helsinki Final Act manifest itself?

Show how the Madrid forum has served America's interest. To what extent has the Helsinki process improved (or hurt) the human rights of the Soviet people? of the people of Eastern Europe? Describe the changed Soviet attitude toward Helsinki.

READING LIST

Basket III: Implementation of the Helsinki Accords, Vols. II and III. Hearings before the Commission on Security and Cooperation in Europe, Washington, D.C., U.S. Government Printing Office, 1977. An invaluable basic document.

Commission on Security and Cooperation in Europe, *Implementation of the Final Act of the Conference on Security and Cooperation in Europe: Findings and Recommendations Seven Years after Helsinki.* Washington, D.C., USGPO, 1982. A useful document.

"Conference on Security and Cooperation in Europe, Helsinki." *Department of State Bulletin,* September 1, 1975. Indispensable as a basic document.

Department of State, *Country Reports on Human Rights Practices.* Report submitted to the Committee on Foreign Relations, U.S. Senate, and Committee on Foreign Affairs, U.S. House of Representatives. Washington, D.C., USGPO, 1983. The introduction provides a basic understanding of the Reagan approach to human rights.

DePorte, A. W., "Europe and the Superpower Balance." HEADLINE SERIES 247. New York, Foreign Policy Association, December 1979. Diplomatic history of the postwar division of Europe into two alliances.

Fascell, Dante B., "Did Human Rights Survive Belgrade?" *Foreign Policy* No. 31, Summer, 1978. Invaluable commentary.

Frankel, Charles, "Human Rights and Foreign Policy." HEADLINE SERIES 241. New York, Foreign Policy Association, October 1978. A focus on the philosophical rationale and scope of human rights and on the ambiguities and the implementation of a human rights policy. Special attention is given to the issue of human rights and détente.

Hearings Before the Commission on Security and Cooperation in Europe. Washington, D.C., USGPO, 1982. An indispensable current source.

Madrid CSCE Negotiations, 1980–81: Selected Documents. Washington, D.C., USGPO, 1982. Excellent source material.

Russell, Harold, "The Helsinki Declaration: Brobdingnag or Lilliput?" *American Journal of International Law,* April 1976. An important legal analysis.

Skilling, Gordon H., "CSCE in Madrid." *Problems of Communism,* July–August, 1981. An excellent survey.

"Symposium: Human Rights and the Helsinki Accord—A Five-Year Road to Madrid." *Vanderbilt Journal of Transnational Law,* Spring–Summer, 1980. Entire issue contains valuable series of essays by specialists on selected subjects.